Extremely WEIRD

FROGS

Text by Sarah Lovett

John Muir Publications
Santa Fe, New Mexico

Special thanks to
Dr. John W. Wright, Natural History Museum of Los Angeles
Alexis Schuler, Curatorial Assistant, Museum of Southwestern Biology, University of New Mexico
Mark Jennings, Research Associate, Department of Herpetology, California Academy of Sciences
Roy McDiarmid, Curator, Fish and Wildlife Service, National Museum of Natural History, WA, D.C.
Tom Dvorak, Jaspar Glass, and Pete's Pets, Santa Fe
Miriam Sagan, Robert Winson, and Isabel Winson Sagan
Tim, Julian, and Sophie Thompson

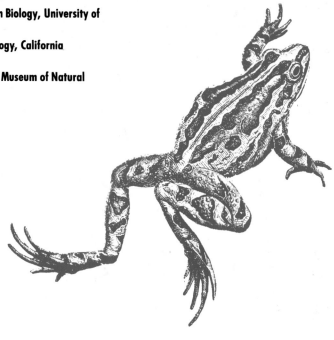

John Muir Publications, P.O. Box 613, Santa Fe, New Mexico 87504

Second edition. First printing February 1996

Library of Congress Cataloging-in-Publication Data
Lovett, Sarah, 1953–
   Frogs / text by Sarah Lovett ; [illustrations, Mary Sundstrom,
Sally Blakemore]. — 2nd ed.
    p. cm. — (Extremely weird)
   Includes index.
   Summary : Describes the habitat, appearance, and behavior of a
variety of unusual frogs.
   ISBN 1-56261-282-4
   1. Frogs—Juvenile literature. [1. Frogs.] I. Sundstrom, Mary,
ill. II. Blakemore, Sally, ill. III. Title. IV. Series: Lovett,
Sarah, 1953– Extremely weird.
QL668.E2L68 1995
597.8—dc20
                                   95-50830
                                      CIP
                                       AC

Illustrations: Mary Sundstrom, Sally Blakemore
Design: Sally Blakemore
Typography: Copygraphics, Inc., Santa Fe, New Mexico
Printer: R. R. Donnelley & Sons

Distributed to the book trade by
Publishers Group West
Emeryville, California

Cover Photo, courtesy Animals Animals © Michael Fogden

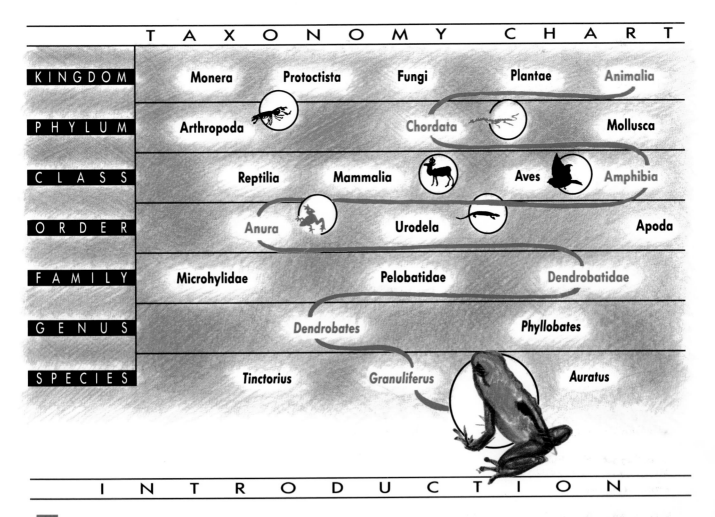

KINGDOM	Monera	Protoctista	Fungi	Plantae	Animalia
PHYLUM	Arthropoda		Chordata		Mollusca
CLASS	Reptilia	Mammalia		Aves	Amphibia
ORDER	Anura		Urodela		Apoda
FAMILY	Microhylidae		Pelobatidae		Dendrobatidae
GENUS		Dendrobates		Phyllobates	
SPECIES	Tinctorius		Granuliferus		Auratus

INTRODUCTION

F rogs are amphibians, which means they live in water and on land. All amphibians depend on their outside environment for body heat: they are ectothermic. That's why you might see a frog sunbathing on a lily pad. (Mammals like us, however, have a constant internal body temperature.)

All frogs are four-legged tailless animals with smooth or warty skin that is usually moist. They never have scales, and they never have claws on their toes. Many types of frogs deposit jelly-like clusters of eggs in water. The eggs hatch into a larval (tadpole) stage. There are lots of different kinds of frogs, about 3,700 species, and frogs live almost everywhere in the world.

Scientists use a universal system to keep track of frogs and the millions of plant and animal species on earth. The system is a science called taxonomy. It's really a way of grouping or classifying things. We use classification systems everyday. For instance, we know there's a difference between a rattlesnake and a zucchini. And we know that a chicken and an eagle have something in common. That's basic taxonomy.

Taxonomy starts with the 5 main (or broadest) groups of all living things, the kingdoms, and then divides those into the next group down—the phylum, then class, order, family, genus, and, finally, species. Members of a *species* look similar, and they can reproduce with each other. For an example of how taxonomy works, look at the highlighted lines above to see how the red and green dart poison frog is classified.

In the pages that follow, look for the scientific name in parentheses after the common name. The first word is the genus; the second word is the species.

Turn to the glossarized index at the back of this book if you're looking for a specific frog, or for special information (what's metamorphosis, for instance), or for the definition of a word you don't understand.

RED-EYED TREE FROG *(Agalychnis callidryas)*

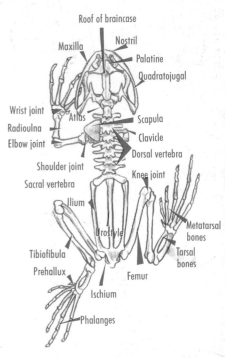

What's neon green and has blue racing stripes, orange toes, a creamy belly, and blood-red eyes with an elliptical or catlike pupil? The red-eyed tree frog, of course. This little tree frog hangs out at night (which means it is nocturnal) in the tropical forests of Central America. With long, sticky toe pads resembling small suction discs and opposable first and second fingers and toes (they can touch each other), the red-eyed tree frog can grasp twigs and branches like a high-flying monkey. This acrobatic ability comes in handy to avoid predators, devour insects, and even to impress a potential mate.

A male in search of a female will call from his perch on the branches hanging high—sometimes fifty feet high!—above a quiet stretch of water. A responsive female will join him, lay a clutch of fifty-or-so eggs on a leaf, and protect them with a thick layer of jelly. When tiny tadpoles hatch, they squirm their way out of the jelly and drop into the water far below. There, they grow for several months before the change into froglets is complete.

Frogs and toads are anurans, a type of "tailless" amphibian. Anurans have a basic anatomy that varies only slightly from species to species.

Frogs aren't the only animals that metamorphose, or change, into a different form during their lifetime. Butterflies metamorphose from caterpillar to chrysalis to butterfly. There's even metamorphic rock—rock that under pressure, heat, or chemical action, has changed its original structure.

F R O G S

Photo, facing page, courtesy Animals Animals © Stephen Dalton

The Quick Change Artist

PAINTED REED FROG *(Hyperolius marmoratus)*

The South African painted reed frog and its 200 or so related species might be called quick change artists—they can change their colors without changing their skins. A painted reed frog could be black and pink one minute and yellow and black the next. That's because their skin is extremely sensitive to changes in light, temperature, and humidity, as well as to their own state of excitement.

Reed frogs eager to attract a mate will sport their full colors. But when they are exposed to bright lights, their skin will temporarily fade to a paler shade.

Reed frogs live among the water plants near lakeshores. There, they find a perfect hunting ground for gnats, mosquitoes, and other small insects. During the dry season, reed frogs can survive for months in cracks between rocks or in terrestrial burrows. When the rains come, a chorus of male reed frogs will begin calling en masse to attract their potential mates. For this, each will use the vocal sac located beneath his jaw which acts as a vibrating sound chamber. Only male frogs have vocal sacs.

Neg. No. 326621, Courtesy Department Library Services, American Museum of Natural History

Frogs are part of nature's food chain. They eat insects, small mammals, and even other frogs. Because they eat mosquitoes, frogs play an important role in controlling malaria and other diseases carried by mosquitoes. In turn, frogs are eaten by bats, snakes, rodents, and other predators. In fact, there is a type of South African snake that dines only on reed frogs.

Photo, facing page, courtesy Animals Animals © Michael Fogden

F R O G S

EASTERN SPADEFOOT TOAD *(Scaphiopus holbrooki)*

The eastern spadefoot toad, with its huge, protruding eyes and mottled, warty skin, lives in sandy areas in the eastern United States. Eastern spadefoots don't usually have to worry about droughts, although, if necessary, they can live buried underground for weeks, even months. The rainy season brings the eastern spadefoot toad out of its burrow to look for a mate. The males hop or waddle to the nearest pond and start c-c-c-croaking in a very loud chorus. Once a female spadefoot has paired with a male, she will deposit thousands of eggs in strands wrapped around reeds and water grasses. After the male fertilizes the eggs, his job is complete.

It takes anywhere from two days to two weeks for the tadpoles to hatch from the eggs. Tadpoles of the eastern spadefoot toads and their Scaphiopus relatives can be very social and often swim in groups. Herpetologists (scientists who study amphibians and reptiles) think group behavior may make it harder for predators to eat the tiny tadpoles. Lots of moving tadpole tails also stir up the mud on the bottom of ponds, and food particles float up to be eaten.

A relative of the eastern spadefoot toad lives in the deserts of the American Southwest and has adapted to an extremely dry climate. After the late summer rains have come and gone, the desert spadefoot toad digs deep into the earth. The toad doesn't use a shovel; instead, there are special horny spades on the soles of its hind feet that serve as "rototillers." Desert spadefoot toads also secrete a mucous coating that helps them retain body fluids. Tucked away, they live for nine months until the next rainy season arrives.

Photo, facing page, courtesy Animals Animals © Zig Leszczynski

FROGS

THE ASIATIC HORNED FROG *(Megophrys nasuta)*

The Asiatic horned frog from Malaya has a snout to shout about. Bony, hornlike projections over its nose and eyes are so sensitive (almost like electronic sensors) that they keep this horny frog from bumping into things. They also keep other creatures from bumping into it because they provide such good camouflage. With tan-colored, lumpy bumpy skin, the horned frog becomes invisible among the leaves, branches, and twigs on the forest floor where it lives and hunts for food.

Most frogs are carnivorous, which means they eat mosquitoes, flies, gnats, crickets, and other tasty insects. Some carnivorous frogs also dine on small mammals and frogs that are not of their same species. The Asiatic horned frog has such a wide mouth and strong jaws that herpetologists believe it may be a cannibal who eats other Asiatic horned frogs in addition to its usual diet.

The Asiatic horned frog has many Megophrys relatives. Some of these tadpoles have mouths like miniature inner tubes. While their lips skim along the surface of the water, these tadpoles hang upright and cruise along for the ride. Inside their lips, the tadpoles have lots of tiny teeth to scrape up microscopic bits of plants and animals.

F R O G S

GRASS FROG *(Ptychadena anchietae)*

Frogs are "loudmouths" when it comes to defending territory, attracting mates, or sending out an SOS. Frogs of both sexes will make a very loud noise when in distress. Distress calls are usually sharp or shrill sounds that have been known to catch potential predators off-guard, allowing the frogs making all that noise to escape.

Male frogs, using their balloon-like vocal sacs, can advertise their intentions. Scientists recognize three types of advertisement calls: courtship—to attract a mate; territorial—to warn off neighboring males; encounter—when two aggressive males are too close for comfort.

Males of some frog species have a single vocal sac; male South African grass frogs have two. When a male grass frog calls, both sacs fill with air, and they look like double bubbles.

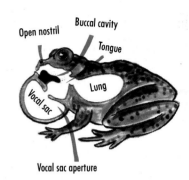

VOCAL SAC DIAGRAM

The International Union for Conservation of Nature has formed a special amphibian group as part of the Species Survival Commission to actively encourage amphibian conservation. If you want to learn how you can help, write: IUCN Species Survival Commission, C/O Chicago Zoological Society, Brookfield, IL 60503.

F R O G S

PANAMANIAN GOLDEN FROG (*Atelopus zeteki*)

Bright yellow means slow down for trouble—the Panamanian golden frog is poisonous (toxic). Like most species of frogs with skin toxins, the golden frog is brightly colored. These are called warning colors. Herpetologists believe that predators learn to avoid frogs with warning colors. Not only are these frogs toxic, they're also noxious, which means they taste bad. After one yucky mouthful, a predator is warned that bad taste goes with bright colors. That's called "learned behavior."

Some frogs are copy-frogs. They look poisonous because of their bright colors, but they're actually harmless mimics. The *Eleutherodactylus gaigeae*, a nontoxic frog, looks almost identical to another, highly toxic frog, *Phyllobates lugubris*. Both frogs have the same skin color and pattern and they live in the same areas, but only one is poisonous. If you were a hungry predator, would you take a chance on a toxic mouthful?

Phyllobates terribilis is one of the largest species of toxic frogs. One *terribilis* contains enough poison to kill about 20,000 white mice.

FROGS

RED AND GREEN DART POISON FROG *(Dendrobates granuliferus)*

Dart poison frogs and their relatives in the Central and South American rain forests come in a rainbow of colors—hot scarlet, neon yellow, and electric blue. They can also be identified by a pair of muscular pads on the upper side of their fingertips and toes.

After the eggs of dart poison frogs hatch, the tadpoles crawl onto one parent's back; whether they choose the male or female parent depends on their species. Who totes the tadpoles?

With red and green dart poison frogs, it's the female, but with torquoise poison dart frogs, it's the male. The tadpoles are then carried to water, where they swim away and must learn to fend for themselves.

Some dart poison frogs are terrestrial, which means they spend most of their time on the ground. Others are arboreal— they live in trees. But all arrow poison frogs need to be near water so their young can develop from eggs to small adult frogs.

Naturalists study the world and its many creatures. Over the centuries, naturalists have developed a system to classify living creatures—how they're different and how they're the same. This way of grouping and classifying is called "taxonomy," and it gives scientists a universal system to keep track of evolution as living things change and develop over time.

The red and green poison dart frog, *Dendrobates granuliferus*, is from the Kingdom: Animalia; Phylum: Chordata; Class: Amphibia; Order: Anura; Family: Dendrobatidae; Genus: *Dendrobates*; Species: *granuliferus*.

FROGS

Captain Hook

EMERALD GLASS FROG *(Centrolenella prosoblepon)*

The emerald glass frog, which lives in Central and South America, is tiny and has "glassy" transparent skin. Most glass frogs are yellow or green, and they range in length from ¾ inch to 2½ inches. Their heads are wide and their eyes small. Glass frogs live in trees and deposit their eggs on leaves above streams. Sometimes the eggs are watched over and tended by the male instead of the female. In many species, the males actively defend the area where they will feed, mate, and raise their young. This is called territoriality and is necessary because natural resources—food, water, vegetation—may be limited.

Emerald glass frogs (and some other species of glass frogs) have a weird, bony spine on their upper arm just in front of the shoulder. This is called a humeral hook or spine, and it's used as a combat weapon to "hook" male challengers. Humeral hooks can inflict fatal wounds on other frogs.

The tropical cane toad, *Bufo marinus*, was brought by humans to Australia, New Guinea, and other islands to eat cane boring beetles and help control sugarcane destruction. Unfortunately, the cane toad hunts at night and cane beetles are active during the day. Now, instead of eating beetles, cane toads eat local frogs. Also, because cane toads are toxic, small animals that eat them die. When humans try to change nature, it's bound to backfire.

F R O G S

PYGMY MARSUPIAL FROG (*Flectonotus pygmaeus*)

The female pygmy marsupial frog from South America carries her eggs in a natural backpack called a dorsal pouch. This tiny frog can tote as many as nine eggs that will take about twenty-five days to develop into tadpoles. Once the eggs are in the pouch, the female carries her precious cargo alone, but she needs help packing her pouch in the first place.

That's the job of the male pygmy marsupial frog. When pygmy marsupial frogs are ready to mate, the male places his toes inside the opening of the female's pouch. As she drops each egg, the male rotates it with his heels and pops it into the female's pouch with his pelvis. Scientists believe each egg is fertilized as it rotates.

Tree frogs have "sticky fingers" or toe pads that grip branches, leaves, and even glass. They can climb the wall with ease.

Ancient Egyptians worshiped the goddess Heket who had the head of a frog. She was a symbol for life-giving change when grain turned into seed and could be planted for food. In India and South America, frogs are worshiped for bringing rain. Asian myths credit the frog with holding the world on its back. Fairy tale frogs, like "the Frog King," often represent our human ability to grow, mature, and become better beings.

FROGS

Photo, facing page, courtesy Animals Animals/OSF © Michael Fogden

TURTLE FROG *(Myobatrachus gouldii)*

How do frogs know that dinner is ready? Do they see it, hear it, or smell it? That depends on the frog. Woodhouse toads are attracted to insects by the sounds they make, and some cannibalistic frogs listen for the sound of dinner calling, croaking, or ribeting; the South American horned frog and other "sit-and-wait" strategists like to see their prey. Scientists believe turtle frogs are attracted by smell to the termites they love to eat.

When turtle frogs are ready to mate in the deserts of Western Australia, females approach calling males above the ground. Together, they burrow underground (sometimes as far as 1 meter, about 3 feet) and remain for five or six months before the female finally deposits her eggs. The eggs are tended underground, and when they hatch, fully formed froglets appear.

Scientists believe that ancient relatives of the turtle frog were present in Australia, Antarctica, and parts of Asia as long as 140 million years ago.

Bizarre broods! The gastric brooding frog is a relative of the turtle frog. Female gastric brooders carry their eggs in their stomach. There, the tadpoles develop. When they are ready to hatch, the female opens her *mouth*, and froglets hop out. Because of this unusual brooding ability, scientists have tried to study this frog. Sadly, the gastric brooder is endangered, perhaps extinct.

FROGS

SPATULATE NOSED TREE FROG *(Triprion spatulatus)*

The spatulate nosed tree frog (from Central America) is casque-headed. In other words, it has a big flat head and a beakish nose that makes it look like a tiny alligator. Thick ridges of skin and tiny surface bones give this frog its unique look (and its name). An extra-large nose comes in handy when it tucks itself into tight spots between branches and leaves. The spatulate nosed tree frog backs into a hiding place until only its nose pokes out. Because very little skin is exposed to the drying air, this protects the frog from water loss.

This frog likes to move around at night, especially from June to October. These are the months of the rainy season in Central America when it mates and lays its eggs in forest ponds. During long dry months, the spatulate nosed tree frog often tucks itself into tiny bird-made holes in bamboo.

Neg. No. 105860, Courtesy Department Library Services, American Museum of Natural History

Grab your umbrella, it's raining frogs. One Bible story tells about a plague of frogs that covered the whole earth. Stranger things have happened.

The world's biggest frog, *Conraua goliath* (the West African goliath frog), can weigh as much as 10 pounds! Because of their size and muscle power, goliath frogs are long jumpers. People have even entered them in the Calaveras County frog-jumping contest. Partly because they are collected commercially, goliath frogs are now endangered, and efforts must be made for their conservation.

F R O G S

GOLDEN EYED LEAF FROG *(Agalychnis annae)*

Leaf frogs are known for their bright color combinations—blue, pink, orange, and green. The nocturnal golden eyed leaf frog, who lives in the tropical forests of South America, looks at the world through flaming yellow-orange eyes. Its lower eyelids are so thin, they're almost transparent.

Leaf frogs are nearly invisible among the leaves of the tropical rain forests where they live. In fact, some species of leaf frogs reflect near-infrared light, which is very unusual for frogs. Herpetologists believe special skin pigments might provide frogs with camouflage because the leaves around them also reflect infrared light.

Golden eyed leaf frogs deposit their eggs on the undersides of leaves, and after several days, the eggs slide into ponds and puddles below. Golden eyed leaf frog tadpoles are very active. It takes them about six weeks to metamorphose into fully formed frogs.

In lab experiments, herpetologists have found that some tadpole species recognize their relatives. When a three-week-old tadpole, hatched all alone, was moved to a tank where two groups of tadpoles were kept, it swam with brothers and sisters instead of nonrelatives.

26

FROGS

TOMATO FROG *(Dyscophus antongilii)*

The tomato frog from Madagascar is named after its shiny red skin. Herpetologists believe there are very few species related to the tomato frog. Even though little is known about them, many exotic frog species are collected for sale in pet stores around the world. Although these frogs can be raised in terrariums, they are never able to return to their native habitat. There is a wonderful way to study amphibian metamorphosis and help conserve frog populations in your neighborhood. If you live near a pond or stream, you may discover frog or toad spawn (eggs) in the spring. Frog spawn looks like a cloudy lump. Toad spawn is deposited in long strings. Gently collect a very small amount of spawn and some water weeds and keep these in an aquarium (not in direct sunlight) with several inches of water.

Change and dechlorinate the water every two or three days. Fish pellets can provide nourishment for the tadpoles. When arms and legs develop and tails begin to shrink, the tadpoles will need both water and land. There are simple ways to create a healthy frog habitat inside a terrarium. Ask an expert at your neighborhood pet store or school for ideas. Adult amphibians eat moving insects like baby crickets, flies, and beetles. While the weather is still warm, frogs and toads should be returned to the spawning pond and released.

What's the difference between a toad and a frog? Probably nothing! Commonly, what is known as a frog in one part of the world might be called a toad in another. Herpetologists have given up using either name to classify amphibians. Instead, they use scientific names.

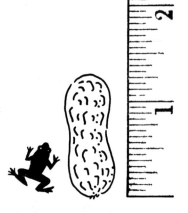

The little grass frog is the smallest North American frog. It's about the size of a peanut.

F R O G S

Guard Frog

GLASS FROG *(Centrolenella orientalis)*

In the forests of Latin America, the male glass frog has the job of "guard frog" looking after the eggs he has fertilized. When the female glass frog is ready to mate, she is attracted to the calling male, and she deposits her eggs on the underside of leaves and fronds where the male fertilizes them. The female is then free to go about her frog business, and the male is left behind to care for the eggs until they hatch into tadpoles. Often, a male will fertilize the eggs of more than one female. In that case, he must look after several broods. Glass frogs grow to a size of about 21 millimeters, which is a little smaller than a 25-cent piece. This particular glass frog is almost see-through and looks a bit like a lime jello mold.

Some insect larvae (or maggots) live as parasites on the eggs of frogs. Eggs that have parasites have an odd shape and will not survive to hatch into tadpoles. Some species of glass frogs with very strong "guarding behavior" will eat damaged eggs to destroy the parasites and save healthy eggs. Look closely at the eggs in this photo. Can you pick out the parasitized eggs in one corner?

FROGS

This glossarized index will help you find specific frog information. It will also help you understand the meaning of some of the words used in this book.